# Garnet and Gray

*Hampden-Sydney Veterans Remembered*

By Colonel Greg Eanes, USAF, (Ret)

*To General Sam*

Greg Eanes

# CONTENTS

# *'Swords Into Ploughshares'*

## Hampden-Sydney College
## Veeterans Day Remarks
## 11 November 2013

Today is the 95th Anniversary of the Armistice that ended The Great War for Democracy better known today as World War I. Memorialized as Armistice Day until the end of World War II when Raymond Weeks, a veteran of the latter conflict, engaged then General Dwight D. Eisenhower for recognition of the day as a National Veterans Day first celebrated in Alabama in 1947. On May 26, 1954 – with a third major conflict in Korea having just ended – now President Eisenhower signed Congressional legislation establishing 'Veterans Day' as a formal day of remembrance.

In so doing President Eisenhower noted the change was made to "expand the significance" of the commemoration so that a "grateful Nation might pay appropriate homage to the veterans of all its wars" noting we should "remember the sacrifices of all those who fought so valiantly, on the seas, in the air, and on foreign shores, to preserve our heritage of freedom" adding that we should "reconsecrate ourselves to the task of promoting an enduring peace" so that the efforts of America's veterans shall not have been in vain.[1]

Again, as our nation has assembled, so does the Hampden-Sydney College community so that it may honor its veterans, both the living and our heroic dead.  Those familiar with the history and the people of this fine institution know that Hampden-Sydney College has been on the forefront of the fight for American liberty literally since its founding at the time of our great Revolution. Could we expect anything less from institution named for John Hampden and Algernon Sydney, the hero martyrs of English liberty?  I think not.

While we will remember those who gave their lives it also fitting on this day to remember those who survived, who returned home, who turned their swords into ploughshares and continued to contribute to their country by their deeds in civilian life. Hampden-Sydney College was built by such men; in part, it was and is nurtured by such men and it has developed such men who have provided and continue to provide principled leadership in private industry and at all levels of government, from local communities to the state and Federal.

The public record of this college is impressive.[2]  The original trustees were literally founding fathers of our Republic.  These included:

A Virginia Militia Colonel named **Patrick Henry**, Virginia's vicar of liberty who spent most of his time in Virginia fighting the good fight in his own backyard yet having a National level impact in the

---

[1] **Title 3-The President, Proclamation 3071, Veterans Day 1954. See the Federal Register Vol 19, No. 198, October 12, 1954.**
[2] *Bulletin of Hampden-Sydney College, Vol. III, No. 4, November 1908, General Catalogue of Officers and Students, 1776-1906;* **Bulletin of HSC, 'A List, with Brief Record of the Alumni and Students of Hampden-Sidney College, Va Who Served in the World War', 1920; Military Times Valor Database http://projects.militarytimes.com/citations-medals-awards/;** *2002 Esther Thoams Atkinson Museum display of Broad Stripes and Bright Stars: A Tribute to Hampden-Sydney Alumni of World War II.*

birth of this nation. There was also, **Robert Lawson** of Prince Edward County. In addition to being a Charter Trustee of this college, he was officer in Virginia's Continental Line in the early northern campaigns before being named Brigadier General of Virginia Militia. In that capacity he commanded the Virginians at Guilford Court House and at Yorktown. Lawson was a member of the Virginia House of Delegates and a delegate to the Convention of the Commonwealth of Virginia on the adoption of the Federal Constitution. In June 1788, he sided with Patrick Henry and voted against adoption of a Constitution that had no Bill of Rights. The leadership of these Virginians ensured that today we have inviolable Bill of Rights.

College alumni **William Henry Harrison** went on to tame the frontier of old Northwest at Tippacanoe and in the War of 1812 at the Battle of Thames. Of course, he became the ninth President of the United States.

*A Summary of Hampden-Sydney College Alumi between 1776 and 1908* reflect no less than three Generals in the service of the United States and 637 Hampden-Sydney men in Confederate service. Those in Confederate service included three Generals, 19 Colonels, 155 officers of other ranks[3], 47 Surgeons, 23 Chaplains and 390 privates and NCOs. At least 83 died in the service.

Hampden-Sydney's sacrifice continued into World War I where records indicate over 400 Hampden-Sydney men served in the uniformed services as privates, non-commissioned officers and officers. Additionally, there were 110 members of the Hampden-Sydney unit of the Student Army Training Corps[4] and 14 Faculty and officers. Many of these Hampden-Sydney men were cited for

---

[3] **Twenty Majors, 73 Captains and 62 Lieutenants. One of the Chaplains was the Rev. Theodorick Pryor, Class of 1826, a power in the Presbyterian Church who was the chaplain of Longstreet's Corps.**
[4] **The Student Army Training Corps was the forerunner of the Reserve Officer Training Corps. For background on the SATC see http://www.dartmouth.edu/~rotc/satc.html.**

distinguished wartime service[5] in France. Among these were:

**Walter Grey Dunnington, Jr, Class of 1911**, was a 2nd
Lieutenant with the 10th Field Artillery, in the U.S. 3rd Infantry

Division. He was wounded and gassed
in July 1918; returned to duty and was
gassed again finally being evacuated 25
October. He was hospitalized for over
a year and finally discharged as
disabled in 1919. He was awarded the
Distinguished Service Cross for combat
action near St. Eugene[6] on the night of
July 14th. According to the citation, he
was "wounded and gassed while
directing the fire of one platoon of his
company under terrific bombardment".
He "refused to be relieved. Although the area surrounding his
position was heavily saturated with gas, he removed his gas mask
in order that he could make his commands heard above the roard of
the guns,".[7] In the post-war period he became a prominent lawyer

---

[5] Others cited for distinguished service are **William Douglas Crawford,
Class of 1914**, Co. C, 102nd Field Signal Battalion and also with the 102nd
French Mortar Battery, 27th Division; **Francis Worth Payne, Class of 1913,**
Co. M, 26th Infantry Regiment. He "distinguished himself by extraordinary
heroism in connection with military operations against an armed enemy of
the United States at Soissons, France on the 19th of July 1918." He was
awarded the Distinguished Service Cross.
[6] During the battle of Chateau-Thierry.
[7] We must also recognize; **Henry Southworth Baker, Jr. Class of 1917**, of
Lexington. He was a private in U.S. Army Ambulance Service serving with
and cited by the French Army's 12th Division and which awarded him the
Croix de Guerre which is only awarded to those soldiers who distinguish
themselves by acts of heroism involving combat with the enemy. Another
noteworthy alumni is **Roswell King, Class of 1909**, of Jacksonville, FL, Co.
G, 104th Infantry then 1st Lt and Captain in the new Tank Corps. He
received three citations and the Croix de Guerre; **William Painter Gilmer,
Class of 1910**, of Pulaski, Va., was a 1st Lieutenat with the 5th Marine
Regiment then serving with the Army's 2nd Infantry Division taking part in
the St. Mihiel, Champayne, Argonne and Meuse-Argonne offensives. He
was decorated with three French Croix de Guerre, a Regimental citation
and two Division citations, including an AEF citation from General John H.

and businessman in New York City. The firm he founded in 1921 still exists on Broadway under the name Dunnington, Bartholow & Miller. Mr. Dunnington died in 1971.[8]

Of the Hampden-Sydney men who served in World War I, at least four were killed in action and eight died of disease or accident.[9] At least seven served as Chaplains and Dr. John Mann, Class of 1894, served as a surgeon with the American Red Cross in Kiev, Russia for six months during the Russian Civil War.[10]

It is estimated that over 1000 Hampden-Sydney men served in World War Two. Additionally, it hosted one of the Navy's V-12 Units to train badly needed officers. While it is impossible to name them all, many returned home to have successful careers where they continued to contribute to their communities. These include:

**Sidney Bruce Spencer, of Farmville, Class of 1937.** The public record shows he was a standout baseball player and team captain in his senior year. He was a Naval officer during the war. He returned home and spent his entire professional career with First National Bank in Farmville eventually retiring as bank's president and executive officer;

**Francis P. 'Moon' Baily, Class of 1943** served in the Army Air Corps. He returned home to Sanibel, Florida where he ran and expanded the family's general store. He became a pillar of his

---

Pershing. Gilmer was a doctor in the Medical Corps and attached to the Marines. The record shows two of his citations were for the Silver Star.
[8] http://www.dunnington.com/
[9] This data was from the 1920 Bulletin. The current list for Hampden-Sydney's World War I dead reflect alumni.
[10] These links provide some background information on the American Red Cross Mission to Russia in 1917. http://articles.washingtonpost.com/2012-01-07/world/35440041_1_russian-children-world-war-trains; http://www.worldwar1gallery.com/russianfront/22523-h/22523_112.html; http://reformed-theology.org/html/books/bolshevik_revolution/chapter_05.htm.

community serving over 22 years on city council and a term as Mayor;

**Phillip Leighton Strader, Class of 1942,** of Lynchburg, Va. He was a Marine Reserve officer in flying 146 air combat missions as a bomber pilot. He was awarded two Distinguished Flying Crosses. He too turned his sword into a ploughshare and became a businessman, a deacon at the First Presbyterian Church, an avid gardner and regular volunteer at the Daily Bread, a charitable organization providing food to those in need;

**James D. Johnson, III, Class of 1939**, of Charlottesville. A veteran of World War II, he later studied film and worked as a documentary filmaker. He was the founding President of the Virginia Film Foundation;

**James M. 'Jimmy Jones', Jr. of Crewe, class of 1945.** He was a bomber pilot and returned to run the family insurance business on the main street for many, many years. He gave back to his community through his work in the Presbyterian church, local civic clubs and by serving on various boards.

**William P. Hay Jr., Class of 1942**, a pilot in World War II, had a distinguished 40-year career as a Judge in the Tenth Judicial District. When inducted into the College's Patrick Henry Society, then President Wilson said Judge Hay "developed a reputation for walking that fine line that assures that justice is tempered properly by mercy."

Among those who did not return were:

**Army Sergeant Chichester Tapscott Pierce, Jr., Class of 1933**, Pi Kappa Alpha, of Lancaster County, Va.[11] was killed in action near Schmidt, Germany, on February 9, 1945. He served in

---

[11] **Pierce was Deputy Clerk of the Court in Lancaster. His survivors include a wife and a two-year old son.**

Company C, 310th Infantry Regiment, 78th Infantry Division fighting across France, Belgium and into Germany.[12]

Private Walter Sapp, a member of his platoon, described the event: "We were making an attack for the high ground northwest of Schmidt on February 9th, when our company was subjected to heavy mortar and artillery fire. At that time Sergeant Peirce was acting as a platoon guide and doing a splendid job of controlling and directing his platoon. I thought I heard a mortar shell coming and I dove  into an old shell hole; just at that moment we were caught in a barrage that hit right on top of us. I raised up quickly and saw Sergeant Peirce falling over backwards and upon investigation found he was killed instantly by mortar fragments." According to the unit Chaplain, "

All of the men in his squad had only the highest praise for the leadership and courage which he manifested under fire." He is a Hampden-Sydney man.

The Cold War and hot wars in Korea and Vietnam likewise saw Hampden-Syndey men. **Brigadier General Holmes Ginn, Jr, Class of 1924** and **Dr. Chapman H. Binford, Class of 1923** served in the Korean War. Ginn had major responsibilities for the medical activities in the field in Korea.[13] He had great interest in

---

[12] October 1943 issue of the HS Record Special Alumni Fund Issue.
[13] He was the 8th Army Surgeon in Korea and contributed to the post-war history, <u>Battle Casualties in Korea: Studies of the Surgical Research Team</u>. He was also instrumental in helping one of his enlisted pharmacist John Fulton at Fort Sam Houston get started in bullfighting. Fulton became Spain's first U.S. born Matador. See

surgical shock and in the use of an artificial kidney for the treatment of patients in shock.

**C. Kendell Hunter, Jr**. of Appomattox, a veteran of the Marines and Air Force served in Korea and Vietnam, receiving two Purple Hearts, two Bronze Star Medals for Valor and four Air Force Commendation Medals. He retired as an engineer with Westinghouse Corporation, was a licensed pilot and a published author.

**Philip G. Padgett, Jr, Class of 1964** was an Air Force veteran in Vietnam. In his post-war period, he worked in the financial industry for more than 37 years and former long-time faculty member Dr. Alan Farrell served in the Army's 5th Special Forces Group in Vietnam where he was wounded in action.

Among those killed in action in Vietnam were:

**Marine 2nd Lt Stephen Francis Snyder, Class of 1965.** In August 1966, he was a platoon commander with Company F, Second Battalion, Fourth Marine Regiment in Quang Tri Province, Republic of Vietnam. He volunteered to lead a force in a night march through the jungle to relieve a trapped platoon. According to the records,

> *"Upon arrival at the besieged platoon's position, he fearlessly took a small group into the trap to assist in evacuating wounded from the enemy-dominated location. Though met with a deadly hail of enemy grenades and small-arms fire, he managed to direct the evacuation of two wounded under the cover of darkness. For the next two hours, with complete disregard for his own safety, he selflessly exposed himself to intense fire while he directed suppressive fires which delayed the enemy assault. When the North Vietnamese finally attacked at dawn, Second Lieutenant Snyder heroically led his platoon in a*

http://sportsillustrated.cnn.com/vault/article/magazine/MAG1081434/1/index.htm

*determined counterattack in an effort to protect the
trapped men. Undeterred by the murderous enemy
grenade barrages and automatic weapons and sniper fire,
he courageously led his men forward until he was
mortally wounded. Second Lieutenant Snyder's stirring
example, exceptional leadership, and marked courage
were the determining factor in breaking the enemy assault
and saved the lives of the trapped Marines."*

He was posthumously awarded the Navy Cross, second only to the
Medal of Honor for combat heroism. Snyder Hall is named in his
honor.

Cold War era alumni and faculty include:

**Marine Major General Gordon Nash, Class of 1971.** He
commanded the Third Marine Division and was Deputy
Commander of U.S. Marine Forces Atlantic. He is now a Senior
Consultant to the Sierra Nevada Corporation and a Hampden-
Sydney College Trustee ;

**Dr. Jim Simms** served in the Marines from 1958 to 1961. As a
company grade officer he commanded a platoon at Okinawa
during the Second Taiwan Straits Crisis when the Communist
Chinese threatened the free Chinese islands of Quemoy and Matsu.
He is now the Elliott Professor of History and oversees the
Military Leadership and National Security Studies Program at the
Wilson Center for Leadership in the Public Interest; and

**Dr. David C. Marion**, a veteran of the U.S. Army and Army
National Guard served as an artilleryman firing 155 Howitzers. He
got out and came to Hampden-Sydney College in 1977 and now
leads the Wilson Center for Leadership in the Public Interest.

There's also **Lt.Col. Rucker Snead, III, Class of 1981** who serves
as the Director of the Wilson Center as well as serving as the Army
ROTC Advisor.

The Hampden-Sydney Alumi of the post-9/11 world have likewise stepped to the plate emulating those who came before them. A review of the website and alumni news gives us snapshots of their stories:

**William Joeckel, Class of 2009** was an Army Specialist and deployed to Iraq, with the 1st Bn, 18th Infantry Regt, 1st Inf Division;

**David Grisdale Class of 2008** became an Army Captain and deployed to Afghanistan with the 10th Mountain Division;

**Zachary Wasmer, Class of 2006** was an Army Captain and served in Afghanistan;

**Major Michael Server, Class of 2003,** joined the Army and served two tours to Iraq as a Black Hawk Helicopter pilot;

Army **Lt. Col. Patrick Howard** and Marine **Lt. Col Chris Hughes,** both of the **Class of 1988**, served in Afghanistan;

There are many others and it is my understanding that at least one Iraq war veteran is a member of the current student body. When their war is over, their leadership and organizational skills and commitment to the public interest will continue to benefit our communities. These are Hampden-Syndney men.

Senior leaders at Hampden-Sydney have also served such as current President Christopher B. Howard, an Air Force veteran of Afghanistan and Wheat Professor of Leadership Studies Lieutenant Genral Jerry Boykin who has been in the forefront of special operations for many years until his retirement in 2007. Both men continue to contribute to the college and other public service causes.

Of course, I cannot end without speaking of Hampden-Sydney College President Emeritus and retired Army **Lieutenant General Samuel V. Wilson** whose 37-year military career took him from World War II through Korea, Vietnam and the Cold War. He also brings us back to a key point about veterans turning their swords into ploughshares to continue to contribute to our communities.

While other men might have 'retired' to the life of a country gentleman, General Wilson demonstrated in a big way that veterans have leadership contributions to make to our country and our local communities. It was after his retirement that General Wilson was instrumental in facilitating the Nunn-Cohen Amendment to the Goldwater Nichols Act establishing U.S. Special Operations Command in 1987. That single act and vision established the foundation for the men, materiel and organizations that would be called upon 14 years later to lead the Global War on Terror after the tragedy of 9/11.

It was also after his retirement that General Wilson formally affiliated with Hampden-Sydney College, first as an Adjunct Professor of Political Science then, at the age of 68, as the 22nd President of the college, and on retirement, as the Wheat Professor of Leadership. As President he even taught Sunday School classes to the students and he taught Sunday School for many years at the Jamestown Presbyterian Church. Though officially 'retired in 2011', President Wilson continues to interact with faculty and students. Having recently turned 90, he now has over 32 years affiliation with this institution. I submit that General Wilson's influence on the young men of Hampden-Sydney College will have long lasting positive influences for our country that will be felt for many, many years as these men work their way into various leadership positions in government and the business community and, as they age, translate what they learned through the mentorship of others.

For over 200 years there has been one continous line of Hampden-Sydney men who have been in the forefront of the fight for American liberty. What we've spoken of today is is but a snapshot.

The surviving veterans of Hampden-Sydney College demonstrated that though they shed their uniforms, they did not shed their civic responsibilities.

They turned their swords into ploughshares.

They continued to contribute to their country and their communities by their deeds in civilian life.

This is the example of our veterans.

Hampden-Sydney College was built by such men;

It was and is nurtured by such men and, thankfully for our nation, it continues to produce such men.

# Portraits of Valor

### November 8, 2015
### Hampden-Sydney College
### In recognition of Veterans Day

On this Veterans Day, in this the 70th Anniversary year of the end of World War II, it is appropriate that we take special notice of those Hampden-Sydney men now enshrined on the famous campus memorial gates who gave up their lives in that great struggle. These were *men of character* who lived *lives of consequence*.[14] They *are* Hampden-Sydney men.

These Hampden-Sydney men made their sacrifices in all the services in the four corners of the world. Those in World War II were in the thick of it from the first weeks of the war until its end. The men I will speak of today are all Virginians; Virginians espousing the chivalric values[15] of honor, courage, integrity, patriotism, self-reliance and a commitment to the Judeo-Christian principles upon which our nation was founded.

---

[14] **A primary mission of Hampden-Sydney College through the Wilson Center for Leadership in the Public Interest is** *"Preparing men of character for lives of consequence."*
[15] **This, in part, is the mission of the Hampden-Sydney Society for the Preservation of Southern Heritage.**

Behind every name is a story; behind every story is an ordinary man who, in his youth, once graced this campus; and behind every man is a family that cared, nurtured and raised the youth into a manhood that was struck down too early by a war he did not want. While time does not allow us to speak to them all, it does allow us to highlight a few of those brave young men of 'garnet and gray' who gave their all in the defense of our republic. These Hampden-Sydney men are _all_ portraits of valor.

**John Francis Blackburn, Jr.,** Class of 1936 was a Harrisonburg  native and the son of John and Alice P. Blackburn. As a Hampden-Sydney student he ran track and was in both the Union-Philanthropic Literary Society and the Valley Club. He was a lawyer at the time of his enlistment on May 29, 1941. Commissioned a second lieutenant Blackburn trained as a tank commander in the 13th Armored Regiment, 1st Armored Division. The unit participated in the landings in North Africa on November 8, 1942 and was in the first American armored division to see combat in World War II. Landing near Oran, they took the city on November 10. By November 25 they attacked an enemy airfield taking it three days later. They repositioned on December 1 and were attacked by German armored forces at El Guessa Heights. This German attack led to a week of fighting that forced the green Americans to retreat to a more stabilized position where they were placed in reserve on 11 December. While Lt. Blackburn's death from wounds is reported as 16 December when the unit was in reserve, it is assessed he was mortally wounded in the earlier fighting. His youngest brother Beverly S. Blackburn was an artilleryman and was also killed in action on April 17, 1945. Both boys are buried in Woodbine Cemetery in Harrisonburg.

**Walter Ray Godsey-** Class of 1939 was the son of Mr. W.M. Godsey of Lynchburg. He graduated from Hampden-Sydney and had been on the *Tiger* staff as Managing Editor, on the Magazine staff and a manuscript editor. While here he also ran track, served as an English Assistant, was on the Debate Team serving as a Virginia Oratorical Representative. He was a member of the Literary Society. On graduation he became a coach at Halifax High School. He joined the Army and was a 1st Sergeant with the 384th Port

Battalion in the Transportation Corps. A Port Battalion was comprised of the Army's longshoremen, railway workers and truck drivers. Their mission was to get the guns, ammunition and other supplies to the infantry and combat arms troops. They were a critical link in any battle. Godsey participated in the North African and Tunisian Campaigns before Operation HUSKY, the invasion of Sicily where he was killed in action on July 11, 1943. While the exact circumstances have not been ascertained, it is likely he was killed by the heavy enemy air attacks which were targeting the beaches and supply ships. Godsey was described by a Hampden-Sydney official who said: *"He was a stalwart young man, a useful first sergeant, and a promising soldier. Many friends mourn his loss, but they are sure that his face was towards the front."* He was a Hampden-Sydney man.

**Henry Spiller Winston III** was the son of Mr. and Mrs. H.S. Winston, Jr., of Henrico County. He was a member of the Class of 1944. While a student at Hampden Sydney College Henry was prominent in athletics and student activities. He was a member of the football squad, the golf team and the Kappa Sigma social fraternity. He was also the vice president of his freshman

class. Henry interrupted studies at Hampden-Sydney to enter the Army in September 1942. He was assigned to the 38th Infantry Regiment, 2nd Infantry Division. On August 5, 1944 while near St. Lo, France Private First Class Henry Spiller Winston, III was engaged in combat with German forces. Severely wounded, he was able to capture some documents. According to reports: *"Suffering from shock and wounds and suffocation he refused to be evacuated for treatment, and insisted on proceeding to his commanding officer with captured documents which contained valuable information. Faithful unto death, he did his duty to the end."* He was reportedly awarded the Silver Star, the nation's third highest award for combat valor. Henry Spiller Winston, III was a Hampden-Sydney man.

**John Brooks Hunnicutt**- of the Class of 1946 was an Army Air  Force Sergeant from Stony Creek, Sussex County, the son of Mr. and Mrs. John R. Hunnicutt. While at Hampden-Sydney, he had been a member of Theta Chi. He had been overseas about seven months as an aerial gunner with Ninth Air Force on a B-26 Medium Bomber. Hunnicutt was described as *"a bold and skillful member of his crew"*. He went out on 35 missions and was awarded the Air Medal for meritorious achievement and faithful performance of duty. Wounded on November 2, 1944, he was in the hospital for two months; returned to combat duty on January 14, 1945 and was killed that very day on a mission over Belgium. A hot metal splinter from enemy anti-aircraft fire struck him in the temple knocking him unconscious. He was flown to a field hospital where he died. According to a Hampden-Sydney official, *"The boy was only nineteen years of age, but he did a man's work and did it well."* This 19-year-old boy was a Hampden-Sydney man. His body was laid to rest in the American Cemetery near Lyon, France."

**George Bruce Williams** was a unique member of the Class of
1944 in that he was partially raised at
Hampden-Sydney. He was the
youngest son of Dr. W. Twyman
Williams, pastor of the church at
Hampden-Sydney. In more ways
than one, this was his home. He was
received in the church at eleven years
of age. He entered Hampden-Sydney
College and became a brother in the
Chi Pi fraternity, served as President
of the Student Finance Board and on
the business staff of the *Garnet* and
the *Kaleidoscope*. He was also a
member of Pi Delta Epsilon, a
journalism honor society.[16] While a junior in college he was called
to duty enlisting in the Army Air Force. In all stages of flight
training he maintained a "superior" rating, the highest given.
Commissioned a $2^{nd}$ Lieutenant in March 1944, he was sent to
bombers. While flying a B-17 in the late summer of 1944 he had
occasion to come near here and made an "air visit" home, passing
over Hampden-Sydney College. It may very well have been his
last visit home. He deployed to England shortly thereafter to begin
combat missions as part of the $331^{st}$ Bomb Squadron, $94^{th}$
Bombardment Group, in the U.S. $8^{th}$ Air Force.

October 7th would be the day of Williams' second combat
mission. The target of the 86-plane B-17 bomber force was the oil
refinery at Bohlen. Approximately, 12 minutes before reaching the
Initial Point (or IP) where they begin the bomb run, overwhelming
numbers of enemy aircraft attacked Williams' Group. His
Squadron took the brunt of the attacks of over 60 German fighters.
According to official reports at the time, *"[Williams'] aircraft was
last seen going down in the vicinity of the I.P. Due to the extreme*

---

[16] **Pi Delta Epsilon merged with Alpha Phi Gamma in 1975 to form the
Society for Collegiate Journalists.**

*battle conditions prevailing, no further observations were made and no further information regarding this crew is known."*

Williams' plane went down about 12:15 in the afternoon and crashed near the German village of Wiehe. Captured German documents indicate the airplane caught on fire, exploded in the air and was 98% destroyed. Sergeant George Perrin was the only member of the crew to survive. He later wrote of young Williams: *"He was a grand pilot and I loved him."*

Williams was a Hampden-Sydney man. He was remembered at Hampden-Sydney in a special memorial service held in the College Church, February 17, 1946.

**James Stafford Martin**[17]- Class of 1931, was the son of James A. Martin of South Roanoke. At Hampden-Sydney, he was a member of the German Club and pledged Theta Chi. He entered service in July 1942, served in Pacific as radio operator and corporal on a B-25 bomber. He was based in Assam Province, India supporting the China-Burma-India Theater of operations. Martin's bomber was on a mission over Burma when his plane and its crew of six men went down in the jungle on October 24, 1944. He was dead at the age of 36. His remains were recovered and are now interred at the Zachary Taylor National Cemetery in Louisville. A memorial marker also exists in Evergreen Burial Park in Roanoke.

**Alfred Lennox Lorraine, Jr**. - Hampden-Sydney Class of 1943 was the son of Mr. and Mrs. Alfred Lennox Lorraine, Sr. of 3009 Sunset Avenue, Richmond, Va. While at Hampden-Sydney he pledged Kappa Sigma and was a member of the German Club and the *Tiger* Business Staff. He joined the Navy and became the pilot of a photographic

---

[17] **No photo available.**

version of the famous Grumman *Hellcat* fighter. His job was to make low level flights over enemy territory to take photographs of targets and potential targets. The film was taken back to the aircraft carrier where Navy photo-interpreters would study the film, identify targets for attack or assess bomb damages after airstrikes. While not an intelligence officer, he was very much a part of the intelligence process.

Lorraine was assigned to Navy Fighter Squadron Fourteen (VF-14), the 'Iron Angels'. Following training, the men of VF-14 reported aboard the aircraft carrier *USS WASP*.

Al's ship passed through the Panama Canal and joined the U.S. Fifth Fleet Task Group 58.2 under Rear Admiral Frank Wagner on May 15, 1944. Four days later they engaged in their first combats with 11 strikes against Marcus and Wake Islands. On June 12, they launched six strikes against Tinian and in following days attacked Japanese positions at Rota, Saipan, Pagin, Iwo Jima and Guam where Al strafed Japanese anti-aircraft guns while flying a photo mission. These missions were in support of the coming invasion of Saipan.

On June 19-20, 1944 Al and his comrades participated in the Battle of the Philippine Sea, also known as the 'Marianas Turkey Shoot' the largest carrier to carrier engagement in World War II and a battle in which the U.S. Navy effectively destroyed Japan's remaining carrier force. The 19th of June had seen heavy combat action in the air, but the Japanese Carrier Task Force was not actually located until a little after 3 p.m. on June 20th. Admiral Mitscher  launched a 230-plane force of Navy Fighters, Bombers and Torpedo planes only to learn about 15 minutes later that the Japanese Fleet was further away than initially reported; literally at the end of the turnaround point for the aircraft. Al Lorraine was part of this aerial task force. They reached the Japanese fleet just before sunset and attacked. Al Lorraine is credited with making *"repeated twilight strafing attacks"* and *"contributed to the damaging of an enemy destroyer which exploded violently amidships."*

By the time they finished, it was dark, and they were low on fuel. The Americans headed back to their carriers. Despite the risk of enemy submarines, Admiral Mitscher made a brave decision to turn on the lights, shine search lights in the air and shoot flares to try to give the American flyers an idea of where the carriers were located so they could get back safely. About 20 aircraft had been shot down by the Japanese. Of the remaining 200, about 80 became lost, ran out of fuel and crashed into the sea. Al Lorraine proved himself to be a superb aviator however and led a group of eight 'lost' planes in total darkness, without modern navigation devices, for a distance of 325 miles, guiding them all back safely to the carrier, with very little fuel left to spare.

For his actions and extraordinary achievement while participating in aerial flight during the Battle of the Philippine Sea, Al Lorraine, was awarded the Distinguished Flying Cross. Yes, he was a Hampden-Sydney man.

Preparing for the invasion of the Philippines Al flew airstrikes against Palau, Southern Mindanao, Visayas, and Morotai. On September 21, 1944, Al and his squadron were making its first carrier based strike against the Philippine island of Luzon. Their attack group consisted of 31 fighters, bombers and torpedo planes. There was only one photographic plane and that belonged to Al. Their target was Japanese shipping in Manila Bay.

Flying over the bay, they could observe 20 large Japanese freighters and oilers with numerous small craft. Seeing the danger, one Japanese destroyer pulled out into the bay where it circled and fired it anti-aircraft guns or 'Triple-A'. The Triple-A was also active in the city and several Japanese fighters from nearby airfields also engaged the Americans.

According to official reports, *"Lt (jg) A.L. Lorraine, Jr. was obtaining photographic coverage of the shipping in Manila Bay escorted by his wingman, Ensign I.D. Lane. He had already made three runs at 11,000 feet over Manila City and along the coast southwest towards Cavite."* On the fourth run, the two planes were slightly west of Manila at 11,000 feet. Ensign Lane was flying about 300 feet above and to the left of Lt(jg) Lorraine when he saw three Japanese Mitsubishi Zeros – also known as Zekes -- flying 3000 feet above them and slightly behind.

The report states,

> *"Ensign Lane immediately opened throttle and according to a pre-arranged signal, flew under Lt (jg) Lorraine to start a weave. As he passed underneath him he started to turn when he saw a Zeke making a run on him. He turned sharply into the Zeke's run and fired, but missed. Another Zeke was now in his sights so he gave this one a 3 or 4 second burst and pulled back up to continue his weave."*

This occurred about 10:05 a.m.

The report said,

> *"Instead of meeting Lt (jg) Lorraine as he expected, Ensign Lane saw him flying in a slight bank to the right. There was a light trail of smoke behind him so Ensign Lane joined up to find out the trouble, and surmised that Lt(jg) Lorraine had been hit in the engine, because his windshield was covered with oil but his hatch was open and he seemed unhurt and had his plane under control. He was then at 10,000 feet... [and] losing altitude slowly. Ensign Lane flew wing on him until they reached 4,000 feet when he decided to gain altitude in order to give Lt (jg) Lorraine better protection."*

> *"As he pulled up he lost sight of Lt (jg) Lorraine under his wing, and immediately made two steep turns, but he could not find him... Ensign Lane called this plane's position to Lifeguard and continued his search for Lt (jg) Lorraine. He*

*was unable to find him. The last time he saw him was
at...1015 [a.m.]."*

The official Navy report had a question about the mission: *"Were
photographs taken?"* The response: *"Yes. Photographic plan did
not return – shot down by enemy fighters."*

Al Lorraine's parents were told five days later that their son was
missing in action. Al was awarded an Air Medal posthumously.
According to the citation,

> *"His assistance in careful planning of the methods employed
> to secure complete photographic coverage, and his personal
> courage, coolness under fire, initiative and determination
> contributed greatly to the success of the operations. He
> evidenced complete disregard for his own safety. His skill in
> leadership, exemplary devotion to duty, and action were in
> keeping with the highest traditions of the United States Naval
> Service."*

Navy LT (jg) Al Lorraine, Hampden-Sydney Class of 1943 was
killed in action. His body was never recovered. Today, in addition
to being memorialized on these gates at Hampden-Sydney College,
he is also memorialized on the Tablets of the Missing at Manila
American Cemetery in the Philippines, the country he helped to
liberate. He was a Hampden-Sydney man.

**Robert Dunn McIlwaine** – Class of
1944 was killed in action in the Pacific on
June 12, 1944. He was a naval aviator
assigned to Fighter Squadron 51, Air
Group 51 on the aircraft carrier *USS SAN
JACINTO (CVL-30)*. Robert was raised
here at Hampden-Sydney College. His
father was the Reverend William Baird
McIlwaine, Jr., Class of 1905. His
grandfather the Honorable William B.
McIlwaine, Class of 1873. And his great-
Uncle was the Reverend Richard McIlwaine, DD, LLD, a

distinguished President of Hampden-Sydney College. Robert enlisted in May 1942 earning pilot wings and a commission in the Navy. During the Marianas Campaign and the battle for Saipan, in an attack on a Japanese ammunition point, his plane took a direct hit from anti-aircraft fire obliterating the plane and the pilot. According to the SAN JACINTO's history, *"Though we had previously suffered operational losses, our first combat loss came on 12 June, when Ensign R.D. McIlwane's Hellcat fighter was shot down by anti-aircraft fire and crashed before the pilot could get clear. Impressive and solemn memorial services were held aboard ship the next day...So far as is known, Ensign McIlwane was the first American pilot to lose his life on Saipan and in the Marianas Campaign."* He was awarded an Air Medal posthumously for his heroism.

**Henry Hunter Watson, Jr,** was a member of the Class of 1938.

He was the son of Henry H. Watson, Senior and his wife Pattie Epes of Crewe. While at Hampden-Sydney he pledged Kappa Sigma. Hunter, Jr. was a graduate of the University of Virginia law school, associated with his father as an attorney and was characterized as a *"promising young lawyer"*. He enlisted in the U.S. Navy on February 26, 1942 and entered the Aviation Cadet Program in April of that year. He trained at Anacostia Naval Air Station in Washington, DC for initial training then Naval Air Station Pensacola for basic and advanced training eventually earning a commission and the wings of naval aviator, graduating in December 1942.

Assigned to Bomb Squadron Two (VB-2) he flew the famous SB2C Curtiss *Helldiver*, a dive bomber. Watson flew the plane but he had a one-man 'crew', Aviation Radioman Second Class Paul E. Flatt of Tennessee. They deployed onboard the *USS HORNET (CV-12)* and were part of Task Force 58 under Vice-Admiral Marc A. Mitscher. To support American amphibious landings in New

Guinea – Codenamed Operations PERSECUTION and
RECKLESS -- Watson and other aircrew were tasked to bomb
Japanese airfields and defensive positions.

Watson's Air Division was tasked to attack New Guinea's Sawar
Airfield in attempt to neutralize Japanese airpower and aviation
fuel and the Sarmi Anchorage to destroy Japanese supply ships.
The *HORNET* sounded General Quarters at 5:34 a.m. on April 21,
1944 with all hands going to battle stations. Poor visibility delayed
aircraft launches. At three minutes after seven in the morning,
Watson and other members of Strike Group 2-A began launching
their attack.

Watson was part of a flight of six dive bombers targeting the
airfield. Flying in at 9000 feet, the bombers dived to within 2,000
feet before releasing bombs ranging in size from 100 to 1,000
pounds. Eyewitnesses recounted at least one large explosion, fire
and black smoke marking hits on the Japanese fuel dump and other
targets. Subjected to anti-aircraft fire, the Navy planes left the area
and headed out to sea to rendezvous for the return trip to the
carrier.

According official Navy reports, one of the airplanes was flown by
LT (jg) Walter E. Finger of Illinois

> *"...overshot at high speed with his wing up, and crashed
> into the plane of LT (jg) Watson. The propeller of LT (jg)
> Finger's plane cut off the forward part of the fuselage in
> front of the wing of LT (jg) Watson's plane and the
> engine...broke off. Both planes...spiraled into the water in
> flames. Two of the planes' occupants (unrecognizable)
> were seen to jump clear but the planes were too low for
> parachutes to open. One parachute opened partially, but
> not sufficiently to break the fall."*

LT (jg) Watson, Petty Officer Flatt, LT (jg) Finger and his
radioman Petty Officer Alfred G. Ponzar are all now memorialized
on the Tablets of the Missing in the Manila American Cemetery in
the Philippines.

The editor of the *Hampden-Sydney Alumni Association Record* said Henry Hunter Watson, Class of 1938, *"...did his duty and he served his country well."* He was a Hampden-Sydney man.

Over 50 Hampden-Sydney men sacrificed their lives in the service of their country in World War II. These were all *men of character*. They all *lived* a life of *consequence*. They are all *portraits of valor* who helped preserve our Republic during its greatest modern challenge.

As we reflect on the sacrifices of these Hampden-Sydney men and so many others not mentioned, I think we can safely say that their experiences at Hampden-Sydney College helped develop their character and, their sense of duty. From them we can take inspiration with the full knowledge that at Hampden-Sydney College, "Honor lives, and tradition never dies."[18]

---

[18] **This is the motto of the Hampden Sydney Society for the Preservation of Southern Heritage.**

Greg Eanes

# Great War Leadership by Hampden-Sydney Men

**Hampden-Sydney College**
**Veeterans Day Remarks**
**9 November 2017**

In this Centennial anniversary year of the United States' entry into the First World War it is fitting that we take time to remember the men from Hampden-Sydney College who served in that conflict. We know over 400 Hampden-Sydney men were involved in the Great War to some degree. When one does a statistical analysis, one can see that Hampden-Sydney men were practically everywhere doing something in support of the war effort. Hampden-Sydney men demonstrated individual leadership, often by example, if not by position and circumstance.[19]

---

[19] **In 1920 the Hampden-Sydney Bulletin published <u>A List, with Brief Records of the Alumni and</u> <u>Students of Hampden-Sydney College, Virginia Who Served in the World War</u> (Richmond: Whittet & Shepperson, Printers) 1920 listing all known Hampden-Sydney men who served in the Great War. This data was supplemented by primary source research.**

**An Overview**
At least 110 Hampden-Sydney men were enrolled in the Student
Army Training Corps while at the college. Of the remaining 369
at least 167 or 45% served in a designated war zone while the
remainder were in the United States or nearby territories providing
training, engaged in training or working in the various medical,
logistical and administrative jobs needed to support an army at
war. Of those serving in the combat zone, at least four were killed
in action and 15 were wounded to some degree.

Most of the Hampden-Sydney men – 276 -- served in the Army
and 139 of these were officers; 69 were in the U.S. Navy, 26 of
whom were commissioned officers and 16 were in the U.S.
Marines, five of whom were officers. At least 14 of these were on
ships at sea in the war zone. At least nineteen served as medical
professionals and eight of these men were medical doctors in the
battle area. Another 18 enlisted men also served in the Medical
Corps. Of those in the battle zone, three of these served with
British Forces.

Two Hampden-Sydney men were from Canada and enlisted in the
forces of their native country and one other man served as a
Liaison Officer with British forces. One man served as an
American officer with the French Army prior to the deployment of
major American forces.

At least two men served as officers in the segregated African-
American units and, of those Hampden-Sydney men serving in
France, six were in the new American Air Service, four as
mechanics and two as pilots.

Seven served as Chaplains, two were civilian employees of the
Young Men's Christian Association serving with the troops, one
served six months as an American Red Cross Surgeon in Kiev,
Russia.

Numbers alone do not tell the individual stories of those who
served on the battlefield and later used their leadership experience

to make a positive difference for their community and, in many cases, for their college. Their units reflect the bravest of the brave.

While time does not permit an in-depth look, it is appropriate we take a few minutes to reflect on some of these Hampden-Sydney men who served on the Western Front during the Great War for Democracy and, where details are available, to see how they served when they came home.

## First In

*AMERICAN RED CROSS HOSPITAL IN RUSSIA-This stock photo is of the hospital staff in Kiev under Dr. Edward J. Egbert who was granted a commission by the Czar as General in the Russian Army. Dr. Mann may be among the group of officers pictured. The Hampden-Sydney graduate was commissioned by the Czar as a Lieutenant Colonel in the Imperial Russian Army. They were visited by Czar Nicholas on one occasion. (Chronicle / Alamy Stock Photo)*

The earliest Hampden-Sydney man in the war zone was **Dr. John Mann, Class of 1894**, a native of Petersburg. Dr. Mann sailed December 16, 1914 to support one of thirteen hospital units funded by the American people for belligerents under the European War

Relief Fund. He reported as the Third Assistant to the Kiev-based Red Cross Hospital Unit 'H' on February 19, 1915.

Dr. Mann was reported to have "an ideal personality and charm – invaluable assets for a doctor" and was commissioned in the Russian military rank of Lieutenant Colonel. Working with a joint American and Russian medical team, they treated Russian wounded. The Doctor recalled

*"Some of the poor fellows had not had their clothes off or a bath for more than six months...These were the fellows who had been all through the campaigns in the Carpathian mountains... Most of them were suffering from frostbite. There was absolutely no kind of gunshot would which we did not have...Some of the cases were horrible, but some of the operations performed by the doctors at times were remarkable. The most remarkable, perhaps, were those on patients who were given artificial jaws."[20]*

After completing a six-month tour he departed on August 8, 1915 for the American St Luke's Hospital in Tokyo where he became the acting Superintendent. The hospital closed a month later having treated over 58,000 wounded Russian soldiers, many often arriving up to two weeks after being wounded.[21] He died on October 31, 1932 in Norfolk, Va after a prolonged illness. He is buried in Blandford Cemetery in Petersburg.

Another early Hampden-Sydney man in the war **Clark Epting Lindsay, Class of 1917**, who left school to join the American Ambulance Field

[20] *The Japan Daily Mail*, September 11, 1915, Vol. LXIV, p122
[21] American Red Cross. <u>Tenth Annual Report of the American National Red Cross</u>, (Washington: 1915); *New Charlotte Medical Journal, V72, p306.*

Service in support of the French Army before the Americans got into the war. Lindsay served in Sanitary Squad Unit One (SSU 1) for a period of six months from 1916 to 1917 earning two Army Corps citations. Each Ambulance section consisted of about 30 men with each section assigned to a French Division, dressed in French uniforms and were treated, for all intents, as part of the French Army.

Lindsay was one of 2,000 American volunteers, most of them coming from one of over 100 American Colleges. As far as can be determined, Lindsay was the only Hampden-Sydney man to serve in this capacity and one of sixteen Virginians to serve in this capacity. He returned home and enlisted in the Army, later serving as a first lieutenant in the Field Artillery.

Another early arrival to Europe was **Alexander Berkeley Carrington, Jr, Class of 1915**.
Commissioned in the American Coast Artillery in October 1917, he was sent to France where he was attached to the French 86th Regiment of Light Artillery serving with them until May 1918 when he was reassigned to the U.S. 34th Artillery Brigade, 55th Ammunition Train, eventually returning home in April 1919.

His family did well in the tobacco industry in Danville and his father served on the Hampden-Sydney Board of Trustees from 1904 to 1934. Lieutenant Carrington followed in his father's footsteps and served on the Hampden-Sydney College Board of Trustees from 1928 to at least 1956 after becoming a banker and later a member of the Board of Trustees of the Dan River Mills; both father and son giving back to their college.

## Army
Fifteen Hampden-Sydney men are identified as having served in the famous 80th 'Blue Ridge' Division which was the only

Division to serve in all three phases of the Meuse-Argonne Offensive. Ten of these men were in the infantry and the remainder served as Engineers, Signalmen or in the ambulance service. The 80th Division deployed in May 1918 and after a period of training was placed into the line with the British near Arras and Flanders along the Somme River. The unit was pulled out to participate in the St. Mihiel Offensive, the first 'all American' offensive in the war and was later employed in all three-phases of the Meuse-Argonne.

Notable among its Hampden-Sydney members was then First Lieutenant – later Captain – **William Perkins (Perk) Hazlegrove,**[22] **Class of 1912**, a Cumberland County native and a Farmville resident. He served with the Headquarters Troop of the 80th Division. As a Hampden-Sydney man Hazlegrove graduated with degrees in Bachelor of Arts and Bachelor of Science and attended UVA law school graduating there in 1916.

In the war Hazlegrove received two divisional and one G. H. Q. citations, the latter a Silver Star Citation upgraded 13 years later to the Distinguished Service Cross, second only to the Medal of Honor in combat awards. According to the citation,

> *"On the night of November 4, 1918, when the left of the division was counterattacked and temporarily driven back from La Thibaudine Farm, though passed by the retiring front lines and under no obligation to remain in advance of them, Lieutenant Hazlegrove and a companion, though having been advised to withdraw, nevertheless, decided to remain and continued throughout the night several*

---

[22] **The name is sometimes spelled 'Hazelgrove'.**

*hundred yards beyond the division outposts in an exposed locality well known to the enemy, where they were swept by cross fire of machine guns and under an intensive artillery bombardment, both by enemy guns and by our own fire. From this position they continued to render reports of hostile movements over a telephone line, maintained at the greatest personal risk, to such good purpose that the attack of the division, renewed on the morning of November 5, 1918, was a complete success. To this voluntary exposure and gallantry in disregard of self is due in large measure the success of the division in carrying out the mission assigned to it.*"[23]

In the post-war period Captain Hazlegrove demonstrated he was also a civic and business leader.    He established the law firm of Hazlegrove, Dickinson & Rea in 1919 remaining the senior partner until his death 60 years later. He served as the chairman of the Roanoke City School Board, served as president of the Roanoke Rotary Club and was president of the Roanoke Bar Association.[24] In 1932 his friends said, *"There is no D.S.C. for citizenship, else 'Perk' Hazlegrove would be in line for one. A busy and capable lawyer, he has never been too busy to respond to the call of service of his church, the*

Hazlegrove '12

---

[23] General Orders No. 6, War Department, 1931; Find-A-Grave

[24] He married Miss Jennie Stouffer and three children, William Perkins, Jr.; Joseph Winston and Wilbur Lee Hazlegrove; The law firm was Cocke, Hazlegrove and Shackleford. This may have evolved into Hazlegrove, Shackleford and Carr; see also his Obituary, page 32, *The Record of Hampden-Sydney College in Virginia*, Vol. 56, No. 1, Winter, 1980.

*Community Fund, the Chamber of Commerce, the Rotary Club, or any other community activity.* "[25]

Captain Hazlegrove died July 2, 1979 at the age of 87. His remains lie in the Evergreen Burial Park in Roanoke under a small nondescript stone that makes no reference to his military service or his receipt of the second highest military award for combat valor.[8] His example in life illustrates he was the embodiment of the Hampden-Sydney man.[26]

**FIELD COMMUNICATIONS-Lieutenant William P. Hazlegrove, Class of 1912, was awarded the Distinguished Service Cross for placing himself in the middle of 'No Man's Land' and sending back vital intelligence by telephone during the night November 4/5, 1918 while being subjected to severe and sustained artillery and machine gun fire.**

---

[25] *The Rattle of Theta Chi*, December 1932, p23 'Alumnus Awarded Service Cross'.

[26] He is buried in Section 1, Plot 94; His son, William Perkins Hazlegrove, Jr., was a pilot of P-51 aircraft in World War II with the Fifteenth Air Force in Italy. He graduated from UVA law school in 1951 and was recalled to active duty. He was responsible for rescuing a colleague who nearly drowned in a Florida swamp in 1951. On August 13, 1952 his P-47 Thunderbolt crashed near Eglin AFB, Florida where he was training in dive-bombing for the Korean War. See the *Record of the Hampden-Sydney Alumni Association*, Vol. 27, October 1952, p19.

Two Hampden-Sydney men served in the famed 42nd (Rainbow) Division in the 117th Engineer Regiment. Among these were Private **William B. Crockett, Class of 1912** of Wytheville and **Wilbur Cosby Bell, Class of 1900,** originally of Augusta County, who served as the regimental Chaplain.

Three served in the 30th Division. Among them was **John Maxwell**

**Robeson, Class of 1896,** a Farmville native who was serving as a Chaplain.[27] Robeson attained the rank of Major, the highest rank granted a Chaplain and the only National Guard Chaplain to receive that honor.[10] At the age of 41 he participated in the battles of Ypres, Flanders, the offensives of September and October 1918 and was wounded in action at Roisell, France on October 24, 1918.

He had previously served along the Texas and Mexico border in 1916 during the hunt for Pancho Villa and later became the rector of St. Paul's Episcopal Church in Lynchburg. He died March 25, 1957 in Orlando Florida after a brief illness being 80 years of age.

Sixteen Hampden-Sydney men are known to have served with the famed 29th 'Blue and Gray' Division. Of these, four served with the 104th Ammunition Train, eight with the 111th Field Artillery and four in the 116th Infantry. While the infantry elements participated in the Meuse-Argonne Offensive, many of those men in the Ammunition Train and Field Artillery did not see action. While their units had been moved to the forward area, the war ended before they received orders for front line duty.

---

[27] **Robeson was born June 30, 1877 in Farmville; married Ellanora Meredith on June 25, 1902 had the following children: John Maxwell Robeson, 18 Dec 1903; Ellen Jaquelin Robeson, 30 Jan 1905; Anna Robeson, 25 May 1908 and George Maxwell Robeson, 11 August 1911.**

Three Hampden-Sydney men served with the 82$^{nd}$ Division in the 327$^{th}$ Infantry, one of the first American units to see combat at St. Mihiel. Among these was a career soldier, Lieutenant Colonel, and later full **Colonel Bryan Conrad, Class of 1891**, of Winchester, Virginia. His life too is the embodiment of the Hampden-Sydney man and the Soldier-Scholar.

Conrad's military service begins before the Spanish-American War when he enlists in 1892 as a private in a local company from Utah where he was practicing law. When the war with Spain broke out he was commissioned a 1$^{st}$ Lieutenant with the Montana Volunteer Infantry seeing active service during the Philippine Insurrection. He later transferred to the regular army as part of the 18$^{th}$ U.S. Infantry which was also engaged in counterinsurgency operations in the Philippines.[28] At some point he gets transferred to the 15$^{th}$ Infantry and sees action during the Boxer Rebellion or China Relief Expedition. By the time the Americans arrive in France, he is a Lieutenant Colonel in the 327$^{th}$ Infantry Regiment, 82$^{nd}$ Division. While records indicate he was badly wounded in a combat action there are no details.

He retired sometime after the war at the rank of Colonel and became active in Hampden Sydney affairs and in co-authoring a 1937 biography on General James Longstreet, appropriately titled JAMES LONGSTREET, LEE'S WARHORSE. This is a standard work on Longstreet and still referenced. At the request of the famous Douglas Southall Freeman, Colonel Conrad read Freeman's entire manuscript of the biography of R.E. LEE, a four-volume work exceeding 2,000 pages. No small task.

Colonel Conrad died in June 1953 at the age of 83. His remains now rest in Arlington Cemetery.

**Clyde Everett Shedd, Class of 1916**, of Bluefield, Mercer County, West Virginia was a First Lieutenant when he was killed during combat operations. Graduating from the Oakland College of Medicine and Surgery in May 1917 he immediately enlisted and

---

[28] **Company M, 1$^{st}$ Montana Infantry**

entered the Army Medical Corps. Following training he was assigned as a Surgeon to the Second Battalion, 327th Infantry and sailed for Europe on April 25, 1918. One news report said, "Upon arriving in France he volunteered for frontline first aid surgery." His request was approved, and he was reported to have been "in the thick of battle" participating in the battles of St. Mihiel and the first phase of the Meuse-Argonne offensive getting wounded on October 15. Rather than recuperate longer he returned to duty on October 16. He was killed that day. He was 25 years of age. His body was laid to rest at Fleville, France, on the day of his death.[29]

## Air Service

Six Hampden-Sydney men were in the American Air Service, two as pilots with the remainder as mechanics. One of these men was **Carrol DeWitt McClung, Class of 1915**, of Greenbrier West Virginia.

McClung was shipped to France in 1918 at the age of 25. Following training was recommended on May 4, 1918 for promotion from Cadet to First Lieutenant in the Aviation Reserve. He served on the front for two months. At 0930 on the morning of November 6 First Lieutenant McClung was scheduled to be in a flight of eight airplanes in the 28th Pursuit Squadron for a morning reconnaissance patrol[30] over enemy lines. Only three aircraft were able to conduct the patrol, those of Lieutenant Stenseth, the patrol leader, and Lieutenants McClung, and Ben. E. Brown. At 10:55

---

[29] See also the *Brattleboro (VT) Daily Reformer*, Nov 30, 1918, 'Lieut. C.E. Shedd Killed in Action'

[30] The reconnaissance patrol was to be at 2,000 meters altitude along the line from Lisle en Barrois, Dun sur Muese, Stanay, Souilly, to Foucaucourt.

[14] He was reported in the hospital on November 8[th.]. See *Gorrell's History*, attachments for 28th Aero Squadron and Third Pursuit Group, entries for November 6, 7 and 8, respectively.

a.m. near Vilosanes Lieutenants Stenseth and McClung observed and engaged a German fighter which eventually crash-landed rolling over on impact. The Americans were simultaneously jumped by five enemy fighters during this engagement. Lt. Brown crashed and became a prisoner of war. Lieutenant McClung engaged one enemy Fokker aircraft. His plane went down but it is not clear if it was due to mechanical failure or because of the combat action. He was posted as 'missing' but later the next day was reported at Evacuation Hospital No. 6 at Souilly. He was said to be 'slightly injured'.[14]

McClung was publicly credited for shooting down four enemy aircraft during his active operations. At the time of his death on June 19, 1938, he was a manager at the Williams Distributing Agency in Clarksburg, West Virginia. Had formerly been associated with a refrigerating firm and operated a store in Lewisburg. He died at the age of 47 while undergoing an appendicitis operation and is buried at the 'End of the Trail' Cemetery in Rupert, West Virginia.[31]

## Navy and Marines

Among the Hampden-Sydney Marines was **William Baxter Southall, Class of 1910,** of Jetersville and later Halifax, Virginia, who enlisted in July 1917 and by late February 1918 was serving as a Private with the 76th Company of the 6th Marine Regiment attached to the Army's Second Division.

The 27-year-old was sent to the Verdun Sector the latter part of March. He arrived on lines at Belleau Wood in the Chateau-Thierry Sector, June 1, 1918. On June 15, while in Belleau Wood, he was seriously wounded in the wrist and thigh while in action

---

[31] **Now Clintonville, Greenbriar Co off WV Road 749. Born 24 August 1892; died 19 June 1938**

against the enemy. Hospitalized, he was sent home and honorably discharged for disability from wounds received in action on March 31, 1919

### *MARINES IN BELLEAU WOOD*

--------------------------------------------------------------------------------

In the post-war period Southall served as a staff reporter for the *Richmond Times Dispatch*, working his way into various positions to include columnist, city editor and editorial writer. He was especially well known in Virginia as the originator and writer of a column called 'Father Byrd' which was featured in that paper. He later joined the *Norfolk Virginian Pilot* and was there when taken ill dying on August 13, 1944.

He is buried in Arlington National Cemetery. The *Times-Dispatch* editorial noted, *"Mr. Southall's untimely death, after a long and agonizing illness, has brought sorrow to the Virginians in all walks of life who considered that his personality and his writings had a special flavor, and who feel that in his death, something uniquely Virginian has gone out of the Commonwealth."*

The U.S. Navy provides medical support to the Marines in combat. Among their surgeons in France was **William Painter Gilmer, Class of 1910**, attached to the Third Battalion, Fifth Marine Regiment. This Pulaski, Virginia native attended the Medical College of Virginia after graduating from Hampden-Sydney. With the war, he enlisted and was commissioned a Lieutenant Junior grade in the Medical Corps serving in France from August 27, 1918 to August 1919. He was in the St. Mihiel Offensive and two phases of the Meuse-Argonne Offensive. During the brutal fighting in the later summer of 1918 Dr. Gilmer's heroism and work was recognized by a Regimental Citation, a Second Division Citation from the commanding general and three Croix de Guerre from the France.

After the war he lived in and practiced medicine for 50 years in Clifton Forge, Virginia for the Chesapeake and Ohio Railroad and the Emmett Memorial Hospital. A community leader he served on the Board of Directors of the Mountain National Bank from 1953 until his death in 1978. He was the brother of Dr. Thomas E. Gilmer, Hampden-Sydney Class of 1923, professor emeritus of physics and former President of Hampden-Sydney College.

Our Hampden-Sydney men represented all the military services and many civilian organizations and held a variety of ranks and jobs in the Great War for Democracy. The war covered a very brief period of their lives. Those that survived brought their sense of duty, patriotism and leadership home where they turned their swords into ploughshares and became leaders in their communities. Their lifetime of service is a legacy for us all.

## ABOUT THE AUTHOR

Greg Eanes of Crewe, Virgina is a Wilson Fellow and Visiting Lecturer at the Samuel V. Wilson Center for Leadership in the Public Interest at Hampden-Sydney College. He supports the National Security and Leadership Studies programs.

A journalist, businessman, freelance writer and educator, Eanes retired as an Air Force Colonel in August 2011 after 34 and one-half years uniformed service that included 23 and one-half years active duty. He supported overseas intelligence operations during the Cold War, the Iranian Hostage Crisis, Operations DESERT SHIELD, DESERT STORM, IRAQI FREEDOM and ENDURING FREEDOM. He holds the Bronze Star Medal with an Oak Leaf Cluster for meritorious wartime achievement, two Defense Meritorious Service Medals and the Air Force Meritorious Service Medal also in support of wartime activities.

He has served on the Crewe Town Council, the Nottoway County School Board and was elected Mayor of Crewe in May 2016. He has a Master's Degree in Military History from American Military University and a Bachelor's Degree from Southern Illinois University-Carbondale. He has been certified by the Virginia Courts System as an expert witness in military history and veteran affairs. He speaks extensively on military history related topics particularly as they pertain to Virginia. He has published multiple works accessible through local libraries and bookstores.

He is married to the former Rosanne Lukoskie of Shamokin, Pennsylvania. They have two adult daughters, Amelia J. Eanes and Amanda Eanes Reed, a son-in-law Donald Aaron Reed and two grandsons, Jase Scott Reed and Avery James Reed.

Made in the USA
Middletown, DE
28 December 2017